MICHELE ARNOLD

JOURNAL

WHO GOD SAYS I AM
A BIBLE STUDY

STYLE
MAGAZINE

IN HIS GRACE MINISTRIES LLC

JOURNAL DEVOTIONAL WHO GOD SAYS I AM A BIBLE STUDY STYLE MAGAZINE

© 2022 Michele Arnold. All rights reserved.

Author photograph by Jarod Arnold. Copyright © 2020 All rights reserved.

Images/templates used with permission from contributors via Canva.

Copyright © 2022 All rights reserved.

THE HOLY BIBLE, NEW INTERNATIONAL VERSION®, NIV® Copyright © 1973, 1978, 1984, 2011 by Biblica, Inc.® Used by permission. All rights reserved worldwide.

Unless otherwise indicated, all Scripture quotations are taken from the Holy Bible, New Living Translation, copyright © 1996, 2004, 2015 by Tyndale House Foundation. Used by permission of Tyndale House Publishers, Inc., Carol Stream, Illinois 60188. All rights reserved.

Scripture quotations taken from the (NASB®) New American Standard Bible®, Copyright © 1960, 1971, 1977, 1995, 2020 by The Lockman Foundation. Used by permission. All rights reserved. www.lockman.org

All rights reserved. No part of this publication may be reproduced, stored in a retrieval system or transmitted in any form or by any means, electronic, mechanical, photocopying, recording or otherwise without the prior permission of the publisher or in accordance with the provisions of the Copyright, Designs and Patents Act 1988 or under the terms of any license permitting limited copying issued by the Copyright Licensing Agency.

ISBN - 978-1-7351373-4-6

Published by In His Grace Ministries LLC

Book website: https://inhisgrace.com/boutique/ols/products/journal-who-god-says-i-am-a-bible-study-style-magazine

Dedication

Lilly, you are loved and cherished beyond measure.
With love Aunt Michele

HOW TO USE:

Devotional day: Read the Bible verse. Pray over the verse and your day. Read the text. Study the verse. Meditate, filling your mind with God's truth and His Words. What does it mean to you? You will see beside a few words and phrases an asterisk * this will mean that there is a definition in the dictionary. See dictionary explanation below.

Memory verse: Each day will have the same Bible verse at the bottom of the faithful in prayer page. Read and re-read this verse and memorize it and keep it close to your heart.

Dictionary: Is found in the back of the magazine on page 109-110. Here you will find words and phrases from the devotionals with their definition to gain better clarity and understanding of their intention and meaning.

Questions: There are two questions asked in this space from the day's devotion. Think about them for a while before you respond. There is space below for your answers. Answer honestly, with vulnerability to the Lord. Because He already knows what you are thinking and how you are feeling. Be open and honest with Him.

Speak truth over yourself: This is a place for you to write about who you are in Christ and to remind yourself of these truths.

My thoughts: You can use this space to write what you felt when you read the devotional, or to expand on your answers to the questions.

Faithful in prayer: Prayer requests and praise reports.

Creative space: I intended this space for you to use in any way you feel led. Draw, write, prayers. Anything you are feeling in the moment.

Contents

1	Fearfully and wonderfully made
7	Loved
13	Valuable
23	Daughter of a King
29	Fearless
35	Masterpiece
45	Wise
51	Known
57	Blessed
67	Protected
73	Strong
79	Confident
89	Forgiven
95	Chosen
101	Equipped
109	Dictionary

I PRAISE YOU BECAUE I AM

FEARFULLY AND WONDERFULLY

made;

YOUR WORKS ARE WONDERFUL, I KNOW THAT FULL WELL.

Psalm 139:14 NIV

I praise you because I am fearfully and wonderfully made. David, who wrote this Psalm, was praying to God. He knew God created him. He understood God saw him. That God was there with him through everything that he had ever been through. He understood God made a way for him when he didn't think he had any other way, so he praised God. He worshiped God. He thanked God for never leaving him, even during those times he might not have felt Him near. David knew God was there.

Let's get a better understanding of what fearfully and wonderfully made means.

Fearfully: Fearing the Lord is standing in *reverence and awe, meaning you have a great deal of *respect and honor for who God is, for what He can do and what He chooses to do. God is mighty. He is all-powerful and all-loving.

What fearing the Lord doesn't mean is cowering in "fear", earthly fear, and being afraid of who God is. Earthly fear is full of anxiety. It is full of bad feelings. Earthly fear is feeling as if someone or something is dangerous. But God is the opposite of all of those things. He is a God of love. A God of peace. A God of hope. Isaiah 41:10 NIV says, *"So do not fear, for I am with you; do not be dismayed, for I am your God. I will strengthen you and help you; I will uphold you with my righteous right hand."* I will strengthen you and help you, God says. This is the opposite of what earthly fear is all about.

Wonderfully: God created you and knit you together. He formed you with His own hands. He created you exactly how He wanted you to be. God took His time on you, yes you. He decided how you would look, the color of your eyes, the color of your hair, even how tall you would be. The human body is so complex, but God knows everything about it. He knows how many times your heart beats. He knows how many hairs are on your head. He has counted them, the *Scriptures say. Matthew 10:30 and Luke 12:7. God knows your heart, He has searched it. It's all beyond what you can even imagine. The wonder of who God is and how He has created you.

How can you live a life honoring God for creating you fearfully and wonderfully so? To honor God is to obey His Word and His commands. God wants nothing more than for you to be obedient to Him and the calling on your life. So you praise Him. You praise God with everything that you do. You praise God with everything that you have. You praise Him because you are fearfully and wonderfully made.

"I praise you because I am fearfully and wonderfully made; your works are wonderful, I know that full well." Psalm 139:14 NIV

fearfully and wonderfully made

Questions

What does fearing the Lord really mean?

How can you live your life honoring God for creating you fearfully and wonderfully made?

DATE
_____

Speak truth over yourself

I am Fearfully & Wonderfully made

How are you fearfully and wonderfully made?

_____
_____
_____
_____
_____
_____

My thoughts:

_____
_____
_____
_____
_____
_____
_____

Faithful in prayer

"Be joyful in hope, patient in affliction, faithful in prayer."
Romans 12:12 NIV

1 JOHN 4:16 NLT

Who God says I am

I AM LOVED

WE KNOW HOW MUCH GOD LOVES US, AND WE HAVE PUT OUR TRUST IN HIS LOVE

GOD IS LOVE, AND ALL WHO LIVE IN LOVE LIVE IN GOD, AND GOD LIVES IN THEM.

We know how much God loves us

"We know how much God loves us, and we have put our trust in His love. God is love, and all who live in love live in God, and God lives in them." 1 John 4:16 NLT

In order to understand how much you are loved, you first need to understand what love is. 1 Corinthians 13:4-8a says; *"Love is patient, love is kind. It does not envy, it does not boast, it is not proud. It does not dishonor others, it is not self-seeking, it is not easily angered, it keeps no record of wrongs. Love does not delight in evil but rejoices with the truth. It always protects, always trusts, always hopes, always perseveres. Love never fails."* These attributes of love never fail. We as humans can fail in these areas, but God, He never fails. He promises us He is always there. He promises that His love for us is never ending and never changing. He heals our brokenness and binds up our wounds. He comforts us in a way that only God can. God's patience never runs out, even when we continually do things we know we shouldn't do. God's love for us is kind, not easily angered. He keeps no records of wrong, *"He has removed our sins as far as the east is from the west"* Psalm 103:12 NLT. God always protects us, our trust and hope are in Him. Most importantly, His love never fails.

God loves you for who you were, who you are, and who you are going to be. Nothing you ever do will ever change that. You are loved beyond measure. A love so strong you can't even *fathom. *"And may you have the power to understand, as all God's people should, how wide, how long, how high, and how deep His love is."* Ephesians 3:18 NLT.

We witness God's enormous love for us through the cross. The *Scriptures say that *"For God so loved the world that He gave His One and only Son, that whoever believes in Him shall not perish but have eternal life."* John 3:16 NIV. Think about this for a second. God gave His only Son to die on the cross for you and for me. To take our sin on as His own. Jesus willingly placed Himself in God's will, in God's plan for His life, and ours. And He obediently went to the cross. *"Greater love has no one than this: to lay down one's life for one's friends."* John 15:13 NIV. God is love. *"We know how much God loves us, and we have put our trust in His love. God is love, and all who live in love live in God, and God lives in them."* 1 John 4:16 NLT. God loves you just like this and more. He forgives you. He provides for you. He listens to you. He understands you.

I think that in order to truly feel God's love for us; we need to spend time with Him. We need to read His Word, to really learn and understand who He is and His promises to us.

Questions

In what ways does God show His love towards you?

Why did Jesus willingly place Himself on the cross for you?

DATE

Speak truth over yourself

I am Loved

How are you loved?

My thoughts:

Faithful in prayer

"Be joyful in hope, patient in affliction, faithful in prayer."
Romans 12:12 NIV

Look at the **BIRDS** of the air, they do not sow or reap or store away in barns, and yet your heavenly Father feeds them. Are you not much more **VALUABLE** than they?

Matthew 6:26 NIV

Look at the birds

God created the birds of the air, decided on the colors of their feathers, and even what type of birds they would be. He also provides them with food for their bellies and warm places to live. He ingrained in them who they are and what they are to do to fulfill their purpose in life. They set about their day, busy with the work they need to do to prepare for what is to come. Gathering sticks to make their nests. Gathering food to feed their babies and themselves. All the while understanding what exactly they are to do.

God does all of this and more for you. He has placed inside of you a God-shaped hole. One that can only be filled by Him and Him alone. You were made on purpose for a purpose. To fulfill your purpose, you need to know who God is and who you are in Him. So understanding your value and worth is so important.

Understand that your value is wrapped up in God and not others. You can so easily hand over your value to others when they say things about you and about who you are. Cling to your worth, don't give it away. Hold tight to what God says about you. Who God says that you are. Because God's opinion of you and His thoughts about you is what truly matters. God says that you are more valuable than gold, silver, or rubies. These items are priceless to the world, high in value. This is you to God. You are priceless to Him, valuable. One of a kind.

Matthew 6:26 ends with a question. *"Are you not much more valuable than they?"* The answer to this question is yes. An enormous giant YES! You are valuable. I would have to say that most of you probably do not understand just how valuable you are. I mean, think about it. You can't value something unless you love and care for it deeply. And God, He values you and He loves you something fierce. God created you first and foremost in His image, I might add. God sent His one and only Son to die on the cross for you. He chose you even before He created the entire world. He wrote every day of yours in His book. You are God's masterpiece, His prized possession. You are *set apart and appointed. Understand and know your worth in God. Memorize *Scripture, hold it close so you never lose sight of who you truly are.

"Look at the birds of the air; they do not sow or reap or store away in barns, and yet your heavenly Father feeds them. Are you not much more valuable than they?" Matthew 6:26 NIV

Questions

Is your value wrapped up in God or others? How so?

Who are you in Christ?

DATE

Speak truth over yourself

I am Valuable

How are you valuable to God?

_____
_____
_____
_____
_____
_____
_____

My thoughts:

_____
_____
_____
_____
_____
_____
_____

DATE

Faithful in prayer

"Be joyful in hope, patient in affliction, faithful in prayer."
Romans 12:12 NIV

Creative space

But you are a chosen people, a royal priesthood, a holy nation

GOD'S SPECIAL POSSESSION

That you may declare the praises of him

Who called you out of darkness into

—

HIS

wonderful light.

1 PETER 2:9 NIV

God's SPECIAL possession

"But you are a chosen people, a royal priesthood, a holy nation, God's special possession, that you may declare the praises of Him who called you out of darkness into His wonderful light." 1 Peter 2:9 NIV

I bet when you were little you dreamed of being a princess? Placing your crown upon your head and twirling around and as you do your gown, the most beautiful that you have ever seen, gently wraps around your legs. And as you continue to twirl, your gown flows through the air in such a sight that makes you giggle. As you get older, the dreams of being a princess fade. The twirling stops and your crown sits in a box in your room, all but forgotten about.

Oh sweet one, bring that dream back. Dust off your crown and place it back on your head. Because I am here to tell you that you are the daughter of a King. A princess. *Co-heirs with Christ. *"But to all who believed Him and accepted Him, He gave the right to become children of God."* John 1:12 NLT.

Your belief in Jesus leads to your *inheritance, which is eternal life with Him. Through your *faith, your belief in God, and your confidence and commitment to Him, your *inheritance is protected. It is shielded by God's power. You are marked with a seal, the *Holy Spirit, the moment you accepted Jesus as your Lord and Savior. *"And you also were included in Christ when you heard the message of truth, the gospel of your salvation. When you believed, you were marked in Him with a seal, the promised Holy Spirit"* Ephesians 1:13 NIV.

Knowing your worth in Jesus will allow you to move through this life with purpose. Others will look at you from the outside, but God, He looks at your heart and knows you. So embrace who you are. Be faithful in Him. And when you move with your purpose, God's purpose, amazing things can happen. Because God *made you on purpose for a purpose. He created you, His daughter, to be a witness to others on His behalf.

So I challenge you to place your crown back upon your head and stand up tall and walk through your day knowing that you are His. Knowing that you are the daughter of King who cannot be moved.

Questions

How will you go about your life reflecting that you are the daughter of a King?

How is your inheritance protected?

DATE

Speak truth over yourself

I am the Daughter of a King

What makes you a daughter of a King?

_____
_____
_____
_____
_____
_____

My thoughts:

_____
_____
_____
_____
_____
_____
_____

Faithful in prayer

"Be joyful in hope, patient in affliction, faithful in prayer."
Romans 12:12 NIV

I PRAYED TO THE

LORD

AND HE ANSWERED ME; HE
DELIVERED ME FROM ALL MY

FEARS

PSALM 34:4 NLT

"I PRAYED TO THE LORD AND HE ANSWERED ME; HE DELIVERED ME FROM ALL MY FEARS." PSALM 34:4 NLT

I PRAYED TO THE LORD

In Mark 5, Jesus was walking through a city, and a man named Jairus came to Him. Pleading with Jesus to place His hands on his daughter as she was sick and dying and he knew that with just a touch, Jesus could heal her. But on the journey to Jairus' house, there was an interruption. One that took Jesus' attention. An unknown woman reached out and touched Jesus' cloak, knowing that if she did, she would be healed. And she was healed immediately. Jesus turned around and addressed the woman. He said *"Daughter, your faith has healed you. Go in peace and be freed from your suffering."* v. 34. While Jesus was speaking to the woman who had touched His cloak, people from the house of Jairus came and said, *"Your daughter is dead. Why bother the teacher anymore?"* v. 35. But Jesus, He overheard what they had said, and He told them, *"Don't be afraid; just believe."* v. 36.

Don't be afraid... in the face of fear and *adversity, don't be afraid. But how you might ask? How am I not to be afraid when life happens? When things don't go as planned. When I am terrified of taking that first step. Or I am terrified of a decision that needs to be made. The unknown of it all. I mean, it's hard when you are staring fear in the face to not be afraid. Don't you think? When you face a world of uncertainty, fear for some can be front and center. Fear, if unchecked, can consume you to the point of not being able to do anything. Your fear is all that you think about, and the anxiety that follows swallows you whole. But Jesus says, *"Don't be afraid; just believe."*

Jesus knows the outcome. He knows your fears. He is there with you in the middle of your fear, calming you, speaking to you, and comforting you. Trust in Him today, sweet one. Know that you don't have to be afraid. Know that your *faith will move you beyond your fear. That your *faith in Him will lead to a calmness within you, one that you can only explain comes from Him and Him alone. The Lord is telling you to calm your spirit because He will take care of you regardless of the situation. So calm your nerves and listen to God's voice. Seek the Lord today and He will deliver you from all of your fears.

Questions

What fears are you allowing to take over today? How are you responding to those fears?

How can you allow your faith in God to combat your fears?

DATE

Speak truth over yourself

I am Fearless

How can you be fearless?

_____
_____
_____
_____
_____
_____

My thoughts:

_____
_____
_____
_____
_____
_____
_____

Faithful in prayer

"Be joyful in hope, patient in affliction, faithful in prayer."
Romans 12:12 NIV

FOR WE ARE GOD'S masterpiece

HE HAS CREATED US ANEW IN CHRIST JESUS, SO WE CAN DO THE GOOD THINGS HE PLANNED FOR US LONG AGO.

Ephesians 2:10 NLT

God's masterpiece

"For we are God's masterpiece. He has created us anew in Christ Jesus, so we can do the good things He planned for us long ago." Ephesians 2:10 NLT

What do you see when you look in the mirror? Do you see a girl standing there staring back at you? Someone who knows all of your thoughts and feelings. Your deepest fears and your greatest regrets, to your happiest of memories. Someone who knows how you truly feel about yourself. As you look back at the girl in the mirror, you might think is my hair is too flat, too frizzy, too thin, or too thick? Or what about I'm not tall enough, or I'm too tall? I wish my eyes were a different color. Or I want that long blond hair like my friend over there. We are good at nitpicking ourselves, aren't we? For me, growing up it was my calves are too big. I could never fit into those cute boots that would go up to the knee, you know, the ones I'm talking about. I was also born with my feet turned out, so my dad and mom had braces placed on my feet to straighten them out. But guess what, my feet needed to be turned out and my calves needed to be strong so I could be the best ballerina that I could be. God knew what He was doing when He created me. And He knows exactly what He was doing when He created you.

Within knowing all of your thoughts and all of your self-proclaimed flaws, the girl staring back at you smiles, because she knows God loves her. She knows God knows her. If only the one whose reflection is showing understood exactly what she knew. She knows God knows her and He sees her. There were no mistakes made when God created you. Trust me when I say that God sees no flaw in you.

So I ask that you stop for a moment and look at yourself, really look at yourself, through the lens of God, and see what He sees. After all, you are His masterpiece. Crafted together by His hands. God created you to be you. He created you to be just the height that you are. Just the right color of eyes and hair. Nothing out of place. God does everything for a reason and a purpose.

Now don't get me wrong, you are not perfect; you will make mistakes, we all do, because we all fall short of the glory of God. But you serve a perfect God. A God who has extended *grace and *mercy towards you. A God who forgives even your biggest sins. But we will get into more of this during the forgiveness chapter. Understand when I say that as God made you, He knew everything that you would say and do, yet He called you His masterpiece, anyway. God Himself handcrafted you. Wow!! How amazing is that?

How can you then move forward in life knowing that you are God's masterpiece? For starters, take what the world says, what the media says, and discard it. You are God's masterpiece. Created in Christ Jesus to do good works. Set out for all to see. God has a purpose for you. One that He has prepared in advance just for you. So embrace who you are. Self-proclaimed, flaws and all. Stand up with your head held high, knowing that you are His masterpiece.

Questions

How can you move forward in life knowing that you are God's masterpiece?

What do you see when you look at yourself through the lens of God?

DATE

Speak truth over yourself

I am God's Masterpiece

What can you say to yourself to remind you that you are God's masterpiece?

_____
_____
_____
_____
_____
_____
_____

My thoughts:

_____
_____
_____
_____
_____
_____
_____
_____

Faithful in prayer

"Be joyful in hope, patient in affliction, faithful in prayer."
Romans 12:12 NIV

"He saved us, not because of the righteous things we had done, but because of His mercy. He washed away our sins, giving us a new birth and new life through the Holy Spirit."

Titus 3:5 NLT

creative space

The fear of the

Lord

is the beginning of

wisdom,

AND KNOWLEDGE OF THE HOLY ONE IS UNDERSTANDING.

PROVERBS 9:10 NIV

Beginning of wisdom

When you think of being wise, what do you picture? I picture a man with a monocle; you know those glasses that only cover one eye, wearing a very nice suit with an *ascot, sitting in a very regal chair. Haha!! *Wisdom, godly *wisdom encompasses far more than that. Far more than how one looks or how much they know.

The *Scriptures tell us that the fear of the Lord is the beginning of *wisdom. Fear of the Lord is a healthy *respect, *reverence, and awe in who God is and what He chooses to do. In honoring who God is, we begin to understand His sheer power and might. Knowledge of the Holy One is understanding. We start to understand just exactly who He is. What His promises are. What He expects from each one of us and how we are to act and react in any given situation.

Being wise is not only about knowledge of a certain topic or subject. Or having good judgment in a situation. Being wise, the *Scriptures tell us, is also to be first pure, then peaceable, gentle, open to reason, full of mercy and good fruits, *impartial and *sincere, James 3:17. You are to make the best use of your time, Ephesians 5:16. Meaning don't waste your days being lazy. Do something, work with your hands, learn something new, *cultivate what you are passionate about. You are not to be foolish, Ephesians 5:17. Make good choices. Listen to the advice and the instruction of others, Proverbs 19:20. Not of people who are quick to get into trouble, but those who believe in who God is. Godly, wise counsel, the *Scriptures say. Being wise means you know when to hold your tongue, Proverbs 29:11. Being wise means you are cautious and turn away from evil. You are not reckless or careless, Proverbs 14:16.

In one of his letters to the Colossians, Paul tells them that his goal for them is that they are encouraged in heart and united in love, so they can have a complete understanding of the mystery of God, which is Christ. Paul goes on to say that in Christ is where you will find *wisdom and knowledge.

So don't go looking to the world for *wisdom or knowledge. Look to Christ. Follow His Word and His teachings. Gain a better understanding of what being wise is all about by *meditating, filling your mind with God's Word. Romans 12:2, NLT says; *"Don't copy the behavior and customs of this world, but let God transform you into a new person by changing the way you think. Then you will learn to know God's will for you, which is good and pleasing and perfect."* Allow God to transform you from the inside out. Soak in every aspect of who He is. Think like He thinks, act as He acts, and you will learn of what God's will is for you. His good and pleasing and perfect will.

"The fear of the Lord is the beginning of wisdom, and knowledge of the Holy One is understanding." Proverbs 9:10 NIV

Questions

What is the difference between being worldly-wise and Godly wise?

How do you gain Godly wisdom?

DATE

Speak truth over yourself

I am Wise

In what ways are you wise?

My thoughts:

Faithful in prayer

"Be joyful in hope, patient in affliction, faithful in prayer."
Romans 12:12 NIV

BUT WHOEVER

LOVES GOD

IS KNOWN BY GOD

1 Corinthians 8:3 NIV

KNOWN BY GOD

Have you ever just sat there longing for someone, anyone, to know you. The real you. Your heart. The love that you can share. The humor that you have, perhaps afraid to let it out because you don't want to make a fool of yourself in front of others. To laugh so hard that you have tears streaming down your cheeks, you know the laugh that is so silent you think that a sound will never creep across your lips ever again. But then suddenly the loudest, most annoying, hilarious noise emerges, just to make you laugh even that much harder. Yeah, that kind of laugh. To find someone with whom you can laugh just like this with, but also be able to open your heart up to them. All without judgment. Someone who will laugh and cry right along with you.

Finding this person is so important to your walk with the Lord. A friend that you can trust and rely on in and through everything. Someone who knows your joys and your sorrows. Someone who knows you.

Trust me when I say that even when a friend like this has come and gone, or not yet found, or sitting here with you today, God is there. God knows you, the real you. He knows your heart. In fact, God searches your heart. He knows every inch, every feeling, every wish and whim. The *Scriptures point to many instances of God knowing you. But I would like to touch on Psalm 139. David is crying out to the Lord. He talks about how God knows his thoughts, how God sees when he sits and when he rises. God knows what you will say even before you say it. God is with you wherever you go. God created you. Piece by piece He made you. With His own hands, He crafted you into who He wanted you to be. God wrote all your days in His book, the day He created you.

God knows you. The real you. Know this, know the truth about how precious and wonderful you are to Him. Know that He loves you and understands you better than anyone else could.

"But whoever loves God is known by God"
1 Corinthians 8:3 NIV

What are some other verses that talk about God knowing you?

Do you have a friend that you can trust and rely on in and through everything? If yes, how will you continue to cultivate this friendship? If no, what steps will you take to pursue such a friendship?

DATE

Speak truth over yourself

I am Known

In what ways does God know you?

My thoughts:

Faithful in prayer

> "Be joyful in hope, patient in affliction, faithful in prayer."
> Romans 12:12 NIV

The Lord bless you and keep you; the Lord make His face shine on you and be gracious to you; the Lord turn His face toward you and give you peace.

NUMBERS 6:24-26 NIV

What does *blessed really mean? When one thinks of blessings, they might think of things, such as a home, a new cell phone, clothes, tangible things that they can touch, smell, and feel. Does God bless in these ways? Yes, I believe He does. However, being *blessed means to be favored by God. Now, this does not mean that God plays favorites or loves someone more than someone else. It means that God is with you all the time. It means that God isn't going anywhere regardless of what you do or don't do. It means that God's love for you is never ending. That your belief in Him is enough to carry you through life's struggles and temptations. In Matthew 5:45 NIV it says *"that you may be children of your Father in heaven. He causes His sun to rise on the evil and the good, and sends rain on the righteous and the unrighteous."* Meaning even if you believe in Him, amongst the joy and happiness, your life won't be without trials or heartache. But His promises say that you are favored, *blessed and loved!

Remember, you are favored by God. In knowing who God is, you gain a sense of peace and hope. In Matthew 5:3-12 Jesus is talking to His disciples. With heartache comes blessing, with *meekness comes blessing, with a hunger and thirst for *righteousness comes blessing, with *persecutions comes blessing. With purity comes blessing, with *mercy comes blessing, with being a peacemaker comes blessing. What Jesus is saying here is if you know Me, truly know Me, blessing will flow regardless of the situation. Because Jesus blesses and favors those who love Him and follow closely after Him.

So we might need to reframe our thinking to reflect God's blessings. God's blessings that are truly different from the worlds. To understand and know that within any circumstance, as long as you know who God is, blessings will abound. God pours out His favor on those who believe. And His favor might not always translate over to the tangible. Often, the intangible is far greater and definitely more comforting. When you can feel the presence of God within you, surrounding you, and encompassing you, can smile regardless of the situation and know that God is right there with you during it all. And when you are walking with the Lord, you become content, fulfilled, at peace, *blessed.

The Lord bless you

"The Lord bless you and keep you; the Lord make His face shine on you and be gracious to you; the Lord turn His face toward you and give you peace." Numbers 6:24-26 NIV

Questions

What does blessed mean? Expand in your own words.

Are you content, fulfilled, at peace, blessed? If yes, explain. If no, explain.

DATE

Speak truth over yourself

I am Blessed

How are you blessed?

_____
_____
_____
_____
_____
_____
_____

My thoughts:

_____
_____
_____
_____
_____
_____
_____
_____

Faithful in prayer

"Be joyful in hope, patient in affliction, faithful in prayer."
Romans 12:12 NIV

"I have been crucified with Christ and I no longer live, but Christ lives in me. The life I now live in the body, I live by faith in the Son of God, who loved me and gave Himself for me."

Galatians 2:20 NIV

Creative space

BUT THE *Lord is faithful* AND HE WILL STRENGTHEN YOU *and protect you* FROM THE EVIL ONE

2 Thessalonians 3:3 NIV

"But the Lord is faithful, and He will strengthen you and protect you from the evil one."
2 Thessalonians 3:3 NIV

HE WILL PROTECT YOU

In 2 Thessalonians 3:2, Paul is talking about being delivered from evil people, saying that not everyone has *faith. Not everyone believes in the *gospel. Not everyone is faithful. The world is full of people who will hurt you and disappoint you. But the Lord is faithful. He is reliable, trustworthy, and He will fulfill His promises to you.

I think we often think that once we believe that nothing bad will ever happen again. Because I believe, because I pray, God has to make everything easy going. No stress, no complications, no heartache, no pain, right? Oh, how I wish this to be true. But it's not. Now, this does not mean that God doesn't protect us. He does. Oh, sweet one, He does. God sees the bigger picture, the one that you can't see, or possibly understand. He knows what you need to wander through in life to become who you need to be.

God promises that He will use what they intended for evil for good. *"You intended to harm me, but God intended it for good to accomplish what is now being done, the saving of many lives."* Genesis 50:20 NIV. Nothing with God is wasted. He will use every experience that you have to shape you and to refine you. Once you believe and are saved, you are marked with a seal, the *Holy Spirit, a deposit guaranteeing your *inheritance. Ephesians 1:13-14 NIV. Your *inheritance is eternal life with the Father. God protects your *inheritance through your *faith in Him. 1 Peter 1:5 NIV.

You need to be an active participant. How you might ask? By *faith, through *faith, you are saved. Your *faith is a belief that God exists. Confidence in Him. A trust so deep that it can't be shaken. Loyalty and commitment to God. By spending time with the Father, reading His Word, you find that your trust and commitment to God becomes easier and easier. God is faithful, even when others are not. God gives you the tools needed to ward off the enemy and keep you safe from his fiery arrows. Trust in the Lord today, sweet ones. Trust that He is right there, walking the path with you. Holding you up and protecting your *inheritance.

Questions

Does God allow a no stress, no complications, no heartache, no pain kind of life? Why not?

How can you be an active participant?

DATE
_____

Speak truth over yourself

I am Protected

How has God protected you?
_____
_____
_____
_____
_____
_____
_____

My thoughts:
_____
_____
_____
_____
_____
_____
_____

Faithful in prayer

"Be joyful in hope, patient in affliction, faithful in prayer."
Romans 12:12 NIV

I CAN

DO ALL

THINGS

THROUGH HIM WHO STRENGTHENS ME

PHILIPPIANS 4:13 NASB

I CAN DO ALL THINGS

Paul wrote 13 of the books in the New Testament, possibly more. Paul says that he learned to be content in everything, in all situations. He knew what it was like to live a life of *abundance and a life of need. Paul understood that his strength was not his own. His strength came from the Lord, and with God, Paul says ALL things are possible. Paul learned to trust God through every high and every low in his life. He praised God throughout. Leaning on God for comfort, for strength, and peace.

Strength is the ability to withstand any trial, a *quiet resolve. Sometimes you might not feel strong, and you know what that's all right. It gives you the ability to press forward in times of struggle. Having strength does not mean that you don't cry, that you don't hurt. That life doesn't get messy. It means that you have God on your side and with Him, ALL things are possible. So you pick yourself up and you dust yourself off and you move forward into wherever you are being called. Hurt and all. God can and will use your hurt to help grow you. He will use your hurt to refine you. God will also use your hurt to help others. *"who comforts us in all our troubles, so that we can comfort those in any trouble with the comfort we ourselves receive from God."* 2 Corinthians 1:4 NIV.

"I can do all things through Him who strengthens me" Philippians 4:13 NASB

I love to say that our strength is not our own. When you spend time with God and you know God, His strength passes through you. His strength holds you up. You couldn't do it on your own. When you allow God to enter in, His strength that passes through you will overshadow your burdens and you will find yourself better able to handle any situation that comes your way. But you have to be *diligent in your prayer life. *Diligent in Bible study. *Diligent in spending time with God. In doing so, much like Paul, you will learn to be content in any and all circumstances. Because it is not what the world can give you, or what you can get, it's all about what you can give to God. If one believes and trusts in the Lord, His *grace and *mercy will follow.

Questions

How can you be content in all situations?

What can you give to God?

DATE
_____

Speak truth over yourself

| I am Strong |

What makes you strong?

_____
_____
_____
_____
_____
_____
_____

My thoughts:

_____
_____
_____
_____
_____
_____
_____

Faithful in prayer

"Be joyful in hope, patient in affliction, faithful in prayer."
Romans 12:12 NIV

But blessed are

THOSE WHO TRUST IN THE

Lord

and have made the Lord
their hope and confidence.

———

JEREMIAH
17:7 NLT

BLESSED ARE THOSE

Confidence is a funny thing, don't you think? I say this because we can lack confidence, but still do things that require confidence. Growing up, I would say that I lacked confidence in myself. But I would get up on a stage in a heartbeat and perform. Even though I had thoughts of not being good enough taking up space in my head. I always seemed to remember the dance routine. My feet moving in time with the music, my costume twirling about as I danced across the stage. The *exhilaration of a job well done. Others seemed to notice. I got solo after solo, moved from an *apprenticeship to *corps de Ballet within months. I say this not to brag, but to explain that what we see within ourselves is often not what others see in us. If I could have only seen in myself what others saw, if I could have only seen what God saw, if I could have understood where my confidence really came from, I think I would have treasured it and *cultivated it far more than I did.

It wasn't until later, much later, that I learned I needed more confidence in the Lord. Because my abilities did not come from me, they came from Him. Yes; I was the one who had to work hard to get where I was. I was the one who had to make the choice every day if I was going to go to class or not. If I was going to put my all into the day, into the sometimes *mundane routine of it all. I needed to place myself smack dab in the middle of the *Scriptures. To read and learn God's Word. To gain a better understanding of who God was and what He had done for me. My confidence came when I understood my worth in who God called me to be. When my confidence is lacking, I remember it was God who called me according to my purpose. And if I continue to rely on Him and know that He will equip me to do what He has called me to do, then my confidence rises again.

The same is true for you. Even though God has gifted you with a certain skill doesn't mean you don't work at it and work hard. God still requires you to put in the needed work for the task at hand. God requires you to do your part. And when you can say to yourself that you put your all into what He has asked of you, you can rest easy knowing that you have partnered with the One who holds it all. You have partnered with the One who extends such *grace and *mercy, who says come to Me, trust in Me, have confidence in who I Am, have *faith in Me, and know that I Am God.

Find your confidence in God today, sweet one. Understand that He believes in you. So go boldly about your tasks. Go confidently out into the world, knowing who you are and Whose you are.

"But blessed are those who trust in the Lord and have made the Lord their hope and confidence" Jeremiah 17:7 NLT

Questions

What has God gifted you with? Explain.

How are you going to cultivate and use this gift?

DATE

Speak truth over yourself

I am Confident

List ways that God has given you confidence.

My thoughts:

Faithful in prayer

"Be joyful in hope, patient in affliction, faithful in prayer."
Romans 12:12 NIV

"I am leaving you with a gift—peace of mind and heart. And the peace I give is a gift the world cannot give. So don't be troubled or afraid."

John 14:27 NLT

Creative space

If we confess our sins, he is faithful and just and will forgive us our sins and purify us from all unrighteousness.

1 JOHN 1:9 NIV

Through Jesus, your sins were paid in full when He died on the cross. When you confess, *repent, and restore, God forgives you, but He doesn't stop there. God removes your sins from you as far as the east is from the west. *"He has removed our sins as far from us as the east is from the west."* Psalm 103:12 NLT. God chooses to remember them no more.

God is faithful and just. He will forgive all of your sins if you will just confess them to Him. Not only will He forgive you, but He will also *cleanse and purify you.

He is faithful and just

I know it's hard to admit when you make a mistake. But it is so freeing once you do. Because carrying around a secret sin can weigh heavily on your heart. When you finally release everything to God, this frees you from having to carry around the guilt and shame.

Even though God has and will forgive you of your sins and will no longer remember them, understand that you can still have very real consequences for your actions here on earth. Your actions, most of the time, will not go unnoticed. You will need to rectify your actions with action, with *restoration, in whatever way that looks. But the beauty in it all is learning and moving forward with the lessons you have gained and the grace and mercy of our all-knowing, all-loving God.

Within God forgiving you, you must also forgive others. In Matthew 18:21-22 NLT, Peter goes up to Jesus and asks Him; *"Lord, how often should I forgive someone who sins against me? Seven times?" "No, not seven times," Jesus replied, "but seventy times seven!"*. Meaning that your forgiveness is unlimited.

Forgiveness does not *absolve the other person of their wrongdoing. It does not give them permission to hurt you. It does not say that what they did was right. Forgiveness is more for you. To be in alignment with God's Word and His commands. It also allows you to let go of the hurt and pain, of the heartache and frustrations of the incident, and move forward. God will do a work in you to fully forgive others and to fully forgive yourself.

Forgiveness can be tough, but it is so worth it. If your past sins come up again, or the feeling of unforgiveness creeps in against someone else, pray. Say, "I have already forgiven, Lord, please help me continue forward in forgiveness." God is there to guide you and to lead you, and He brought Jesus down from Heaven and placed Him on this earth as an as an example for all of us to follow.

"If we confess our sins, He is faithful and just and will forgive us our sins and purify us from all unrighteousness." 1 John 1:9 NIV

Questions

What example did Jesus set for you about forgiveness?

Do you have any sins you are holding onto that you need to confess to the Lord?

DATE
_____

Speak truth over yourself

I am Forgiven

How are you forgiven?

_____
_____
_____
_____
_____
_____

My thoughts:

_____
_____
_____
_____
_____
_____
_____

Faithful in prayer

"Be joyful in hope, patient in affliction, faithful in prayer."
Romans 12:12 NIV

I AM CHOSEN

YOU DID NOT CHOOSE ME,

BUT I CHOOSE YOU

and appointed you so that you might go and bear fruit—

FRUIT THAT WILL LAST

—and so that whatever you ask in my name the Father will give you.

John 15:16 NIV

I CHOSE YOU

"You did not choose me, but I chose you and appointed you so that you might go and bear fruit—fruit that will last—and so that whatever you ask in my name the Father will give you." John 15:16 NIV

As I was studying 1 Peter, I feel like I got a better understanding of Jeremiah 29:11 *"For I know the plans I have for you," declares the Lord, "plans to prosper you and not to harm you, plans to give you hope and a future."* When you couple this verse with Psalm 139:16, Jeremiah 1:5, Romans 8:29, Ephesians 1:11, and Ephesians 2:10, you start to see God's plan. You start to understand that you were already known, chosen, *predestined, and *appointed by God.

Think about that, you are chosen, *set apart, *appointed, *predestined, prepared in advance to do the work of the Father. Wow, and amen. What an amazing thought.

There was nothing you had to prove. You didn't have to convince God that you were worthy of the task. He chose you before the foundation of the world, Ephesians 1:4. Think about this for a moment. You were chosen, *set apart, *appointed, *predestined, prepared in advance before God even uttered the words *"let there be light."*

God has chosen you to bear fruit, good fruit, fruit that will last. John 15 starts with Jesus talking about being the vine, God being the gardener, and we are the branches. The vine is what provides the branches with nourishment and life. Jesus, being the vine, is our strength and nourishment. To bear fruit, good lasting fruit, you must abide and remain in Him. Without the vine, the branch cannot bear any fruit. There will be times when God has to prune you. It is not a fun process. But a process that is used to refine you and help you bear fruit that will be sweet, bright, and needed for this world.

The *Scriptures talk about how others will know you by your fruit. We see in Galatians 5:22-23 a list of the fruits of the Spirit. When you *abide in Jesus, really *abide in Him, the fruits of the Spirit will be how others identify you as a Jesus follower.

In this life, there will be times you will be overlooked. Times when others will dismiss you and not appreciate you for being you. But remember, sweet one, that God chose you. He picked you out, handcrafted you, prepared you, and *set you apart. Chosen for just this time in life, to do just what God has asked you to do. You have been *set apart for God Himself. Loved. Cherished. Chosen.

Will you do everything that you can to abide in Him, to walk in a manner worthy of your calling?

What do you want people to see in you?

DATE
_____

Speak truth over yourself

I am Chosen

How has God chosen you?

_____
_____
_____
_____
_____
_____

My thoughts:

_____
_____
_____
_____
_____
_____
_____

Faithful in prayer

"Be joyful in hope, patient in affliction, faithful in prayer."
Romans 12:12 NIV

So that the servant of **GOD** may be thoroughly **EQUIPPED** for every good work

2 TIMOTHY 3:17 NIV

In 2 Timothy chapter 3, we see a stark contrast between those who believe and those who do not. Non believers will be lovers of themselves and other earthly desires. They won't be kind to anyone and they will forget all about God and who He is. And along the way, they will try to get others to follow along with them. As you read through the list of things Paul says non-believers will behave like, you will see things like being disobedient to your parents, ungrateful, unforgiving, lacking self-control, and you might pause and say, well I have been those things. What does that mean for me? First off, it means you are human. You have made some mistakes in life because you are not perfect. However, you will notice Paul says that these people will act as if they know God, meaning they understand and know that there is a God, but they are denying His existence and His power and will in their lives. These people have ignored the truths of God so they can live for themselves. Paul is warning us of such people. In fact, Paul says have nothing to do with these people. As we spoke about people knowing you by your fruit, you will also know others by theirs. Whether the fruit is good and lasting or if the fruit is bad. People will take notice.

Paul says, *'In fact, everyone who wants to live a godly life in Christ Jesus will be persecuted'*. None of Jesus' followers will exit this life without some kind of *persecution against them for their faith. Some won't like that you believe. Some will say it's a crutch. Others will say it's all make-believe. And they will continue to be deceived and continue to deceive others. But when you stand in the truth of who God is and the teachings that Jesus left, you will become equipped to handle these kinds of situations.

Cling to the knowledge of God's Words, for this shall make you wise. Paul rounds out chapter 3 with this; *"All Scripture is God-breathed and is useful for teaching, rebuking, correcting and training in righteousness, so that the servant of God may be thoroughly equipped for every good work."* v.16-17 NIV. The Word of God is living and true. Each and every word placed on the pages of the Bible was placed there with intention and meaning. The Words of God teach you, sometimes they *rebuke you and correct you. Other times, they train you. All so you can be equipped to do every good work. To minister to others and to show them the love of Christ.

God called you, within your calling, God will and is equipping you to do what He has asked you to do. He will not abandon you. He has prepared the way for you. Are you willing to walk in it?

"so that the servant of God may be thoroughly equipped for every good work." 2 Timothy 3:17 NIV

equipped

Questions

What shows up consistently in your life and the life of those you choose to hang out with?

Are you willing to do what it takes to walk in your calling?

DATE
_____

Speak truth over yourself

I am Equipped

How has God equipped you?

_____
_____
_____
_____
_____
_____
_____

My thoughts:

_____
_____
_____
_____
_____
_____
_____

Faithful in prayer

"Be joyful in hope, patient in affliction, faithful in prayer."
Romans 12:12 NIV

"O Lord, you have examined my heart and know everything about me."

Psalm 139:1 NLT

Dictionary

Abide: To dwell, remain

Absolve: Set free from blame

Abundance: A large amount of something

Adversity: Difficulties

Apprenticeship: Someone in training for a certain position

Appointed: Decided on beforehand. Set aside, specifically selected

Ascot: Type of men's tie

Blessed: Favored by God

Co-heirs: Sharing an inheritance with someone else

Corps de Ballet: Members of a Ballet company who dance together in a group

Cultivate: Prepare, work on, developed

Diligent: Intense concentration and focus

Exhilaration: Extreme excitement and happiness

Faith: Is trust in who God says He is and the promises He has made. *"Now faith is confidence in what we hope for and assurance about what we do not see."* Hebrews 11:1

Fathom: Understanding. Contrast, cannot fathom equals lack of understanding.

Gospel: Good news

Grace: Unmerited or undeserving favor - getting what we don't deserve - God's intervention

Holy Spirit: The Holy Spirit is a gift given to you the moment you believe. The moment you place your trust in God. Jesus left you with an advocate, someone to help guide you. The Holy Spirit lives within you, guides you, and prompts you to do the right thing.

Impartial: Not taking a side one way or another

Ingrained: Firmly held, not wavering, deep and permeant

Inheritance: Something that is inherited, passed down from a previous owner.

Made on purpose for a purpose: You were not an accident. You were created by God, formed by His hands with intention. Put on this earth at just this time to do what God created you to do.

Meditating: Filling your mind with God's Word.

Meekness: Humble or gentle attitude

Mercy: Loving kindness, withholding of punishment - not getting what we deserve.

Mundane: Same old routine, often times dull and boring.

Pray: Praying is communication with the Lord. Prayer is not only asking God for things but praising Him for what He has done. For what He will do, and what He chooses to do. Prayer should encompass a time of listening, taking the time to wait on the Lord to respond.

Predestined: Chosen ahead of time. Already decided on by God.

Persecution: To be treated unfairly or cruelly because of your belief in God

Quiet resolve: Firm determination to do something

Rebuke: Extreme disapproval and correction of actions or words

Repent: To turn completely away from sin or wrongdoing

Respect: To hold in esteem or honor

Restoration: To repair something that was broken, in this context a relationship.

Reverence: Deep respect for God

Righteousness: Free from guilt and sin.

Scriptures: God's Word, the Bible

Set apart: Designated for a specific purpose

Sincere: Genuine, honest

Wisdom: Starts with knowing God and trusting in Him. Wisdom is not an inward-facing focus, or selfish. With Godly wisdom, it places your focus on Him. It is not self-seeking, but instead, it is gentle and kind. Loving and pure. Full of mercy and doing good. Recognizing that Biblical values should be first and foremost in your life.

Other Journal magazines

Journal Light for my path a preteen/teenage Bible study style magazine

This Bible study devotional takes on a unique perspective of your traditional Bible studies. Whether it be your first step in learning God's Word or if you have been walking the path for some time, this is a great way to dip your toes into God's Word and who He is. This magazine is aimed at meeting the needs of young people transitioning in their faith from baby believers to maturing adults.

More from in His grace

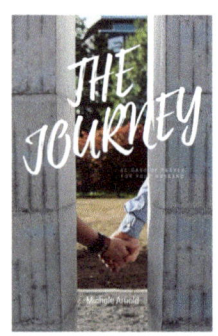

The Journey: 40 days of prayer for your husband

All throughout this devotional are ways to pray over, and for, your husband. We will delve into what it looks like being a wife and a woman of God and gain a better understanding of who we are in Christ. Let's consider some new thinking, based on timeless Biblical principles, contrasted against our current cultural and social norms. We have the life changing opportunity to gain a better understanding of how to move through your marriage and life in general, through God's lens. We have all gone through moments of great joys and deep pains. I pray that the words on these pages fill you with hope, peace, and a sense of who God is, and also, a sense of who you are in Christ.

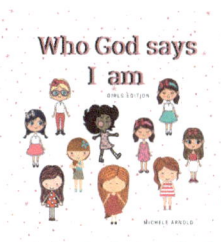

Who God says I am: Girls Edition

I am's are a positive affirmation of who your daughter is in Christ. A gentle reminder of her importance to Christ and the world. When we speak over our children about who they are in Christ they become equipped to handle what the world throws at them. The I am's give your daughters the confidence needed to pursue their calling and help them to know their true identity in Christ.

Who God says I am: Boys Edition

I am's are a positive affirmation of who your son is in Christ. A gentle reminder of his importance to Christ and the world. When we speak over our children about who they are in Christ they become equipped to handle what the world throws at them. The I am's give your sons the confidence needed to pursue their calling and help them to know their true identity in Christ.

Hope "To trust" 21 day devotional

Hope is a word we use too often to express a desire for that which may occur but definitely is not certain. However hope in Christ is a different kind of hope. It is a hope that can be banked on, trusted, and waited for with anticipation that is rooted in promises made and met. There is truly no more uplifting feeling than placing your trust in a hope that can be relied on. When we plant ourselves in God's hope, we can trust He is faithful to finish the good work started in us.

Peace "To be complete" 21 day devotional

Peace is a word we seem to use far and few between, but with God we can experience His peace every day. Even when our circumstances don't seem to align with peaceful feelings, you can be at peace in heart, soul, and mind. There truly is no greater feeling than being in complete peace. When we choose this peace, as God's free gift, we are set free and we are free indeed.

About the Author

Michele Arnold, wife, mother of 2, and Grammy (Grandma) to 1 (for now). In the midst of doting on her grandbaby, Michele runs a small farm with her husband and children. Michele has written, taught, and facilitated Bible studies, one-day workshops, and simulcasts. She maintains and runs In His Grace Ministries webpage where you can find articles about faith, family, devotionals and so much more. Michele is passionate about family, leading, equipping and confirming women about who they are in Christ, following the Lord and His leading in her life and that of her family.

KEEP IN TOUCH

WEBSITE:
WWW.INHISGRACE.COM

FACEBOOK.COM
INHISGRACEMINISTRIESLLC

INSTAGRAM:
INHISGRACE.MICHELE

EMAIL:
INFO@INHISGRACE.COM

"being confident of this, that He who began a good work in you will carry it on to completion until the day of Christ Jesus."

Philippians 1:6 NIV

www.ingramcontent.com/pod-product-compliance
Lightning Source LLC
Chambersburg PA
CBHW041102070526
44583CB00002B/31